SOUVENIR

By Aimee Suzara

WordTech Editions

Published by WordTech Editions

P.O. Box 541106

Cincinnati, OH 45254-1106

ISBN: 9781625490636

LCCN: 2013957260

Poetry Editor: Kevin Walzer

Business Editor: Lori Jareo

Visit us on the web at www.wordtechweb.com

ACKNOWLEDGEMENTS

A first book is a rite of passage, and culminates a long journey of poems being sown and nurtured, with many to help feed them along the way. First to thank is always God, the Higher Spirit, Life, Breath, Diyos, Bathala, that presence with many names. And the Ancestors, whose light shines the way, including Lolo Jose Muyargas, Lola Paciencia Muyargas, and Remedios Muyargas Suratos; Lolo Fructuoso Suzara and Lola Soledad Liñan Suzara. Thanks to my parents, Eleanor and Emilio Suzara, for always believing; to my sister Aileen Suzara. To Toussaint Haki Stewart, for your enduring love. To my dear friends and family.

To those who helped me with drafts, weaving, editing, sparking, considering, digging deep, deciding, and believing in my words, including Elmaz Abinader, Evelina Galang, Luis J. Rodriguez, Ching-in Chen, Tamiko Beyer, Vickie Vertiz, Kenji Liu, Maya Chinchilla, Lisa Marie Rollins, David Mura, Willie Perdomo, Craig Santos Perez, Barbara Jane Reyes, Sharon Bridgforth, Vangie Buell, Kimberly Dark, Avotcja, Juliana Spahr, Genny Lim, David Maduli, Lee Herrick and Ishmael Reed.

Those who have helped hold up my life as a writer and performer, Alicia Kester, Ellen Sebastian Chang, Amara Tabor-Smith, Marc Bamuthi Joseph, Ise Lyfe, Paloma Belara, Dael Orlandersmith, Dorothy Santos. My twin Ramona Webb, my spirit sister Anastasia Tolbert. To Amy Wheeler and Hedgebrook for nurturing the beginning, middle and end, to VONA (Voices of Our Nations) for giving me a place to belong.

To my colleagues and students who inspire me, all the folks at CSUMB, Debra Busman, Diana Garcia, Maria Villasenor, Umi Vaughan, Lauren Muller, Leo Paz, Jeanne Batallones, Catherine Eagan, Karin Spirn. My artistic collaborators, teachers and friends who help me fly, Jen Soriano, Juan Calaf, Ron Quesada, Frances Sedayao, Aimee Espiritu, Stephanie Johnson, Idris Ackamoor, Rhodessa Jones, Fe Bongolan, OACC, PAWA, all the theater and playwriting folks. To my childhood friend Amanda Gustafson, whom I missed all along. To the artistic vision of book designer Marlon Sagana Ingram. To Juan Felipe Herrera for his words in "The Heart is a Hollow."

The content of this book was largely inspired by the work of Abraham Ignacio, Jorge Emmanuel, Enrique de la Cruz and Helen Toribio. My research was supported by the Missouri History Museum; special thanks to Dennis Northcott. The writers of the books whose words and research I drew from, and the photographers whose images I encountered in my own research; and especially, those named and unnamed whose eyes gazed back and told me their stories. To those of you taking the time to listen.

Thank you to the editors who published some of these poems previously in: *580 Split, Lantern Review, Phat'itude Magazine, Konch Magazine, Enizagam, Walang Hiya: literature taking risks toward liberatory practice* (Carayan Books), *Finding the Bones* and *the space between* (Finishing Line Press).

Before this book went to press, Typhoon Haiyan hit the Philippines. To the survivors, our *kababayan*: blessings and resilience.

sou ve nir (s$\overline{oo}$′ və-nîr′)

n.

A token of remembrance; a memento.

SOUVENIR
Table of Contents

EXHIBIT A: The Philippine Reservation

EXHIBIT B: Anthropology

EXHIBIT C: Science

EXHIBIT D: Objects & Artifacts

I can feel myself under the gaze of someone whose eyes I do not see, not even discern. All that is necessary is for something to signify to me that there may be others there.

– Jacques Lacan, *Seminar One*

EXHIBIT A: THE PHILIPPINE RESERVATION

Objects & Artifacts

I enter the air-conditioned room, a maze of glass cases. Here,
a lace-up dress stretched over a headless bust.
White taffeta layers bloom and cascade like a wedding cake.
Between this statue and myself, I see my ruddy face reflected
in the glass. And which is the ghost: this colonial woman,
headless, eyeless in her eyelet dress, or me, gazing back?

In the adjacent case: grey, tarnished krisses; a bolo; the sharp tips
poke my eyes. A headdress with red and black feathers fans the city
out of me. A rice god, elbows on knees, watches, so far from his domain.
Philippine playing cards sleep in a stack. The top one stares back.
My face is framed by the oval shape surrounding its subject: a sightless
boy, holes for eyes, the rice picker's conical hat. Skin like coffee.

He rides an elegant water buffalo. I imagine myself there.
Was this a real boy modeling for the artist? Flies and mosquitoes hovering,
the *kalabaw's* tail swatting, back bristling? Sweat behind the boy's ear,
a desire to be witnessed. And the painter, sent to collect the very best,
a mess of putrid sweat gathering under his thick suit, skin crawling
in the heat. Or was the boy a figment, just one like many others?

If I were there:
1904, a souvenir:
Which suit would I become?
Which number?

FACT: On April 30, 1904, The Louisiana Purchase Exposition, otherwise known as the 1904 World's Fair, opened its doors to the public in Forest Park, St. Louis, Missouri.

Alonney, Angay, Angpeo

FACT: As the Louisiana Purchase Exposition commemorated Lewis and Clark's exploration and Westward expansion in North America, the Philippine Exposition highlighted the United States' recently acquired territory of the Philippines, as "purchased" from Spain via the Treaty of Paris in 1898. The Treaty of Paris and Spanish-American War usually overshadow the Philippine-American War, which persisted for fourteen years.

Ballicas, Balison, Balonglong

FACT: About 1,200 Filipinos were brought overseas from their homes in the Philippines to live in villages on the 47-acre Philippine Reservation.

Caplaan, Caplis, Chainen

FACT: They were arranged into ethnological "types" and required to carry out a semblance of life in their home villages. The "wild tribes" of Igorots, Negritos, Bagobos and Moros were the most popular displays. "Dog-eating" was a well-attended rite performed by the Igorots, amassing the exhibit many awards and large audiences.

Filomena , Kika , Luisa

Catalog of Objects

1 Bahag
1 Skirt
1 Beaded bag
2 Beaded necklaces
3 Carved statues of the rice god
1 Set of Filipino playing cards

You walk into the Missouri History museum. You see white everywhere: alabaster casts of women in Victorian dresses, plaster infused with "staff" from the Philippines. Lion heads and the columns of the Palace of Fine Arts. Victorian men and women sit atop elephants, smiling in tall black hats and mustaches and finely pressed jacket, brown men on either side. The placard marked "Labor" shows Africans and Asians bent over to build, to clean, to make the Fair grand.

You dream that night: statues a creepy feel swimming in dark waters I touch warm flesh underwater underfoot find out they're dead recently dead lots and lots of stairs two six-year-old boys they want me to follow them the bus is waiting I'm lagging like I don't want to go the bus is parked above lots of steps it's really hot moving slow there's a woman who likes me slippers on slippers off I can't find mine now a movie theater and behind the theater a shopping market

2 Bontoc Head Hunters
1 Visayan Girl
1 Geisha Girl
1 Esquimaux Family
1 Hoochie Coochie Girl

You see the daguerreotypes of Filipinos, Native Americans, Eskimos, Arabs, and Japanese, assembled in one cluster on the wall. Nearby, you see playing cards of Filipinos and a beaded Bagobo dress behind the glass case. You see your face reflected in the glass.

THE CALL OF THE WILD!

note: how the white men
study how the white men
studied the brown men
who looked like me.

IN THE LABORATORY OF THE ST. LOUIS WORLD'S FAIR

Each day, they were measured, between 10 am and 4 pm.

NAME Aggos (age 18), Alonney, Angay, Angpeo (age 19), Chief Antonio (Tetepan, elder and leader, age 27), **SEX** Aongay, Apaggnet (age 20), Apoguet (father of child born in St. Louis), **AGE** Asil (age 11), Aspil (age 20), Attao , **SKIN COLOR** Ayhawan (age 25), Baliscao (age 17), **WEIGHT** Ballicas, Balison (age 22), Balonglong (Antero Cabera, age 15), Bayungorin (age 45), **HAIR** Benigna, Lazardo Bibit (assistant), Bocasen (age 26), Bomantan (age 18), Pedro Bonito, **HEIGHT** Bugti, Cbayao (age 32), **EYE COLOR.** Calutin (age 20), Caplaan, Caplis, Chainen, Conegma, Congo (age 26) Acong (age 24), **ARM SPREAD** Amil (age 20), Arsenio (age 26), **STATURE** Badin (age 57), Baja (age 21), **GIRTH** Buleng (age 25), Dabat (age 36), Danani (age 12), **HEAD FORM** Danga (age 32), Datto Facundi (age 36), Leone (age 9), Maldani (age 44), Mandan (age 50) **FACIAL ANGLES** Galo (age 22), **NASAL ANGLES** Gonan-Glali, priest of Pandita (age 48), Lapucni (age 27), **EYE ATTITUDE** Leone (age 9), Maldani (age 44), Mandan (age 50) **CHEST** Andia (age 21), Bihinang (age 22), **BODY AND LIMB GIRTH** Biria (age 1), Filomena (age 40), Kika (age 2), Luisa (age 22), Polonia (age 22), Sebia **RELATIVE LENGTHS OF LIMBS TO THE BODY** Andang (age 45), Basilio (age 25), El Captain Gamot (age 55, leader), **PULSE** Clario (age 25), Gbag (age 50), **RESPIRATION RATES** Humalin (age 35), Jorge (age 12), Jose (age 21), Juan (age 15), Julian (age 2), **LUNG CAPACITY** Kalmen (age 18),   Kamahalin (age 40), Kario (age 25), **DIGITAL AND JOINT MOVEMENTS** Marsia (age 24), Millong (age 8), Pedro (age 2), Rupino (age 42), Sayas (age 23), Tiberio (age 30), **STRENGTH** Tili (age 6), Toyang (age 12), Unda (age 22), Luis Francis Wilson (born in St. Louis July 19, 1904). [2]

With Compliments

Written to the image in Judge, June 11, 1898 entitled:
"Now that I've got it, what am I going to do with it?"[3]

Uncle Sam's
angular hands
curve round
black bum

ankle bracelets of bronze
jangle
to the rhythm of kicks and sobs
lipstick lips outline

black open mouth;
viscous tears
snake over ebony cheeks
over garland of broken shells

over poor Philippine baby
kinky hair and bulbous head
rocking, rocking
paper flapping

on a thread
like a flag or
a morgue tag:
"Philippines

with compliments of Dewey."

Through the generosity of the United States government, which appropriated a million dollars for a Philippine exhibit at the Louisiana Purchase exposition, visitors to the fair will be able to get a keen insight into the manners and customs of the Filipinos, as well as a thorough knowledge of the wonderful resources of this country's new possessions in the Orient.

- *St. Louis Republic*, May 01, 1904

Possession

Flag descends.

We shot niggers and rabbits![4]

A pale hand collects it:
Stripes replace our sun.

This is not war; it is simply massacre and murderous butchery.[5]

At the Philippine Reservation

We roast dogs for your fancy:
the sacred turned to gluttony.

The act of cooking a dog
over a contrived fire pleases you
                    even as you are disgusted
warn the residents to watch their pets
hide gaping mouths
behind starched, lace collars.
Women's ribcages push out
in delight: corsets
nearly bursting.

DEPARTMENT OF EXPLOITATION.
ANTHROPOLOGICAL DIVISION.

You shackle us,
fashion us in your likeness. Some of us in,
some of us out. We stare
at each other: civilized at the savage. Savage

at the civilized. But all that distinguishes us
are these starched dresses, parasols and powder.

an unexcelled collection of
the leading peoples
from Northern Luzon to Mindanao[6]

The Pike is overrun with you,
a swarm of doilied dolls;
your superfluous dresses like
over-frosted wedding cakes.

SKULLS / BRAINS OF IGOROTS / STRAPS, KNOTS, CORDS

You twiddle your mustaches
as though they control the world:

Pear's Soap: a potent
factor in brightening
the dark corners
of the earth[7]

turn us on and off
with every flick and fiddle.

It was delightful when we were tired to sit down and watch the people pass.

– Words of a visitor to the 1904 World's Fair[8]

Philippine Souvenir Card #1

Nine of Hearts.
Upon a kalabaw, I sit
tilling the perpetual rice
paddy of your imagination.
Legs astride, bare-
footed. Painted into
position. My brim
hides my face. You, viewer
would think I have no features.
My skin
only black like the kalabaw.
We stare, eyelessly. Who
are you to shuffle me
into order, bid me away
in games, assign me
to a number, a suit?
My heart thrums beneath this starched
Yellow shirt, I cannot breathe
For its strict collar. Every day
I wake to till this same
Stereotype of a field. It's
Barren now, no rice left
To fill your plates, only this vision
Of a man. You think you've succeeded
in capturing me;
The way I brace my kalabaw with ring,
With whip.

World's Fair Box
At the Missouri History Museum Library

The Negritos are very interesting. The lowest grade of human creatures under the jurisdiction
of the President of the United States, they are more debased in morals, more feeble of intellect
than the Digger Indians of California.   - William Curtis, 1904

At the entrance to the Library guarded by wire-rimmed men, I leave
my belongings in a locker, taking only pencils and notebook paper.
My eyes trace immense dark wood panels, broad, cold tables and rounded
study lamps. The ceiling rises, arched into stained glass. I note the instinct

to clasp my hands in prayer. I hear the whisper of fingers tracing over leather
book covers turning onion-paper, each inhale marking discovery. The Special
Collections Manager, a compact man, takes my index cards scribbled
with numbers from the Dewey Decimal deck. He disappears behind the stacks

into a back room. After a moment, he emerges, saying, *Take a look at these.*
Soon, several books wrapped in archival paper sleeves are piled before me.
A picture box arrives, filled with photos of tribal peoples from 1904.
I lift the cardboard lid; the scent of forgotten dust flies to my nostrils.

I flip through manila folders labeled:
Igorotte.
Negrito.
Visayan.

I select *Negrito,* pull the folder up to see its contents.
A photo falls into my hands. In sepia-tone, there is a nipa hut -
thatched roof and stilted bamboo construction. Crouching
ebony-skinned boys lean bows into their hips readied

for some unseen target. Behind them, an elder man with kinky hair
and full lips stands like a sentinel. At least sixty, he appears stiff
as a bamboo stalk. Refusing the loin cloth, he wears Western clothes:
buttoned down shirt, a fitted suit jacket, slacks. A tipped hat shields

round eyes that almost glow. What does he say to the boys, before
the shutter closes, drawing their shadows into light?
What do the boys reply, as they yank the bows back?
What does the photographer tell them, as they pose?

Is it cold, in this unnamed season? Do the boys' thighs bristle
in their nakedness? Or is it hot, the man sweating in his thick suit
reminiscent of a ringmaster's tuxedo,
tipped hat rimmed with sweat?

Each day, I read: *they demonstrate a ritual at 9, hunt boars and reenact*
the selection of a chief at 10; the women cook in the afternoon;
honor the dead at the close of the day. Each Saturday
they show pale-skinned visitors how to carve a tattoo.

I find the man's name later: *El Captain.*
I hold the aged photo between my fingers,
the yellow of El Captain's eyes a warning.
And all of us viewers vexed.

**In the card file
at the Missouri History Museum Research Library:**

Oral History
In the Listening Room at the Missouri History Museum Research Library

You select an interview subject from the list. You pick William Link. The page is typed, the errors crossed out. You listen to the compact disc, the 1979 voices shrill and distorted.

Now they talk a great deal about these Igorrotes that
they had and their dog diet. I don't know whether they
did or whether that was just a story. [9]

The Igorrotes have always been dog-eaters,
and they consider it not at all strange that
they should eat such food. In fact, they are
but one of many primitive people who relish
the dog at table. [10]

I never saw them eat, and I never saw them prepare a dog, but
some people say that they did.

Because they eat dog flesh, the Igorotttes
aroused the Woman's Humane Society to
protest, but they insist on receiving
their favorite food while at the fair.

You peel open the cardboard box, shake the dust from your hand. A book with its spine undone.

At the fair, people wanted to see how we kept house, ate and even how we slept together.[11]

We'll just have to take their word for that. I watched
them in their native dances, on one occasion, and I was
always looking to find a dog that was going to be roasted
next but the dog didn't appear in the act at all.

Stray canines in the vicinity of their camp
were always in danger of sudden death. So I'd get tired of waiting and I'd go on, but the newspapers reported that it was true, that they did use dogflesh for food. *Olo, our cook, lit a match to start a fire by striking the flint against the side of his foot. That was a feat that made money and for that he stayed behind.* You return the book, thank the librarian, get your stuff from the locker outside. You feel you've forgotten something. You leave with this nagging feeling that something has been left behind.

MHM LRC Stacks

St.L. 711 F76eg
St.L. 606.02 W177s
St.L. 811 Ig24s
907.4 En56

Museum Note #2: What you bring

One loin cloth (no mention of weather).

> Bring what you need for four days. Don't bring those shoes that rub the inside of your right foot, it's too hot in St. Louis and your skin will blister. It's going to be 100 degrees or more. Don't bring all those long-sleeves for Oakland evenings. Bring things that aren't polyester; they will feel heavier in the humidity. Don't bring your electric flosser, it's too heavy. Bring bug repellent. Don't bring too many books. Bring the exact number of underwear and the exact number of socks; you won't have time to wash. Bring notebooks, lots of notebooks. Bring your research. Bring a pencil. Bring the articles you have already read. Read them again when taking the Metro. Bring your smartphone with the google maps and web access.

Embroidered things, woven things, baskets
and exotic tapestries.
Lots of weapons; they like weapons:
krisses, swords and knives;
it brings out the headhunter quality.

It's a performance.

Bring your stage
attitude.

Philippine Souvenir Card #2

Nine of diamonds.
In an oval frame
we stand pert in a row
facelessly, brown skin swathed
in white cotton shirts
buttoned to the neck
(proof we are
Spanish-primed,
American-schooled.)
We are Tagalog but
you forgo tribe and
language - label us
simply "A Native Group."

The Missing Link[12]

THE LOWEST GRADE OF HUMAN CREATURES UNDER THE JURISDICTION OF THE
PRESIDENT OF THE UNITED STATES.

Negrito
Pygmy
hominid between primate and human

ignore the crawling feeling   *fly rubbing its feet together*
                                   torn wings
skin-hairs   eyelash
a moist tickle
epidermis
desire to scour

THEY ARE VERY WARLIKE MOUNTAINEERS. THEY EAT WITH THEIR FINGERS. THEY
HAVE CURLY, KINKY HAIR, AND ARE AFRAID OF THUNDER. THEY DISLIKE TO BE
QUESTIONED. VANITY IS THEIR DOMINANT VICE. THEY REGARD AMERICANS AS
GIANTS, ALTHOUGH THEY ARE THE LARGEST OF THE FILIPINOS. [13]

THERE WAS NOTHING
BEFORE WE ARRIVED.

Museum Note #3

Igorotte Village

note:
obtain artifacts
war booty/skulls/names/
signify the other. *hey.*
it was a long time ago.

Norms [14]

There they tom-tommed and danced the true savage dance and cut the throats of the six dogs, which had been several days fattening. –Missouri Governor Hunt, 1904

We are the White Man's burden –
The Igorotte we're called
A name we do not use at home
But now we must respond.

We do not sharpen teeth like Ota
So you spare us from the animal zoo.
Our display is much more savory:
You've provided all our tools.

From beyond the bamboo rail,
The women gaze and stare –
They like the wind blowing our cloths
Revealing nature's share.

The women hold their breaths
As we balance spear and shield
And in our loincloths, fake a war
Invoking every fear.

The men desire to join us
In our pretended tribal dance;
When they gyrate their awkward hips
We give them our applause.

Our nakedness causes a stir
But brings the tickets in;
You give us woolen trousers
To hide our copper skin;

And then you take them back,
To keep our "authentic" look;
And in our flimsy village
We dance to prove your Book.

You give us twenty dogs a month
To stage a ceremony;
And warn visitors to watch their dogs
In case we get too hungry;

But when you are not looking,
We bury canines in the dirt;
American dogs are much too fatty;
Our stomachs start to hurt.

We play the stage like actors
who know our script by heart;
we laugh at your hypocrisy
and keep our selves intact;

And so we squat and aim our spears
And eat the dogs you bring us;
Until the day we may return
We'll play the savage circus.

So you, the Brown Man's burden –
Keep your dogs on steady tie –
The crackling bones might be your own
If you don't keep us in your eye!

Your new-caught, sullen peoples,
Half-devil and half-child.[15]

Good Boy[16]

This loin cloth is our currency.
We see how the women swoon
how the dance blows the wind
and gives them a little peek.

It's our game of hide
and seek. Welcome
to our hips.

These white men, how stiff and like
a tree they stand, as if
they don't have knees to bend.
They think we laugh to see them dance.
But it's how we survive in this caged existence.

And yet we have learned
to expect no less than thievery
from these men.
They ask for a performance:
that is what they'll get.

They fear their wives may wish
to get behind these stage-curtains.
Maybe we'll dance
the way they never can.

Antero[17]

The Call of The Wild!
Dog-Eating
Head Hunting
WILD PEOPLE
From the Mountain Fastnesses of the Philippine Island!

Gather objects.
Assist anthropologists.
Maintain dignity.

Their star pupil at the American school,
I became a translator, gained high demand.
I bartered travel for trust;
now I help Jenks collect objects and people.

After the humid summers at Forest Park,
I saw the clouds descend on Seattle
and remembered the Cordilleras.
How I miss the red clay earth!
How I miss the rice terraces, shimmering
and the kalabaw, tilling the fields, leaning
and sniffing, their nostrils wet and shivering.

With our eleven children,
Estero and I live the life of performers.
We have learned how to laugh
even when their laughter is at us.

We've grown a second skin; the mask
required to survive in this savage place
where human bones, songs and souls
are trafficked.

The Igorrotes, a group of tribal Filipinos who had been fed a ration of twenty dogs by the city, were whisked away secretly on the night of December 1, 1904, to avoid a court action which might have kept them in St. Louis for show purposes.[18]

– Henry S. Iglauer

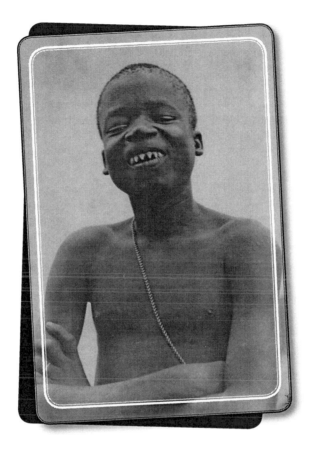

EXHIBIT B: ANTHROPOLOGY

Bushman Shares a Cage With Bronx Park Apes.

The African Pigmy, "Ota Benga."
Age, 23 years. Height, 4 feet 11 inches.
Weight, 103 pounds. Brought from the
Kasai River, Congo Free State,
South Central Africa, by Dr. Samuel P. Verner.
- from a 1906 headline in the *New York Times* and a sign at the Bronx Zoo

African Pigmy   a MAN more than   neglected grave
23 years   civilization's eyes   The Men of Science
4 feet 11 inches   CANNIBAL.   savior complex
103 pounds   you   slave

MISSING LINK

                   Brought from   Dohong the orangutan
                         SAVAGE.   *Kasai River*   Y
                  o   u

          Evolution.   hung a hammock
              at the zoo

      ETERNAL CHILD   you?
   filed off the caps   *Congo Free State*   PRIMITIVE.

~~you~~   jagged teeth

South Central Africa   bullet through   y
o   u
    ruptured heart   never
                     to return   y
y
y
y
y
y
                     y

o
                    u

41

Dear Ota Benga,

I am writing you across a century and this country
where we are both strangers. Why am I disinterring you
to put you in a book next to Antero and El Captain
and the many unnamed subjects made to dance and fight
and craft and speak, show off your teeth, befriend
the very ones who mocked you? Measured each day
to demonstrate that you were the link
between humans and apes.

The skull, nose, cheekbones, shoulders, sternum,
the breadth of your hips, the length of your legs,
your height, your wide and muscled feet,
all of your physique, like ours, taken apart
under the glass, we, living specimens. And the joy the scientists
must have felt to discover "proof" of their superiority! But you
kept faith that even in the most devilish men there was still
something human. Your captor, dubbed savior, who took you

from the Congo, was supposedly a friend. It's not much different
now, Ota, or should I call you Sir, what they likely never granted you,
as they locked you up with the monkeys. Today
we're still measured, mocked. The pictures impossible
to become, unless we should stop eating, peel away our skin,
inject ourselves with whitening drugs, put plastic over our eyes
in unnatural hues; set scalpel to our curves, pump botox into fissures,
we are told to aspire to nothing less than figures of wax,

airbrushed and retouched. We sing American pop songs, always
we can sing and dance. In your later accounts, you fall into depression.
Who wouldn't? Though the photos only show your rows of sharpened
teeth glinting in a Cheshire grin. You hoped to return one day to the Congo.
I imagine how you must have felt. You could never go home,
and preferred to die instead. Who would do otherwise, in your position?
Humiliated in the press, infantilized, demoted to animal by the crowds,
poked and prodded by mustached men in laboratory coats.

But you went down in history:
refusing to continue the life of an animal

trapped far away from home
in a cage
in a Zoo.

Sincerely, xxx

Exhibit at the Alaska-Yukon Pacific Exposition
Seattle, 1909

                              Watch them!

Watch them crouch
on their haunches

                    watch them cook
                    smoke their pipes
                    weave on looms

dark skin gleaming;

watch them!

Go on -
come closer.
They won't hurt you.

                              Watch them!

Aren't they **exotic**?
Headhunters
straight from the Cordilleras
of the Philippines.

They'll make you
a fine cloth
they'll play you
a strange melody
they'll dance
in native costumes
their dark skin gleaming.

                              Watch them!

They won't hurt you!

They can't!
They're behind the rail.
They're not allowed
to mingle

with the spectators.

So watch them
from the safety of your seats
their dark skin gleaming.
They're our winning
exhibition

so please -
enjoy!

water cure: a telegram to 1901 from the future

Get the good old syringe boys and fill it to the brim

lifesource our liason to the sea lessoned on Philippine insurgents stop

attempt to get confession force the feel of drowning stop

cause waterlung/pneumonia cause pleuritis cause adrenaline overload cause irregular heart beat cause release of catecholamines cause heart attack stop

proven despite CIA sanitation of a formal method yes one can be scared to death stop

We've caught another ------- and we'll operate on him

if not from broken limbs or bruises if not oxygen loss if not vital organ failure stop

and under this distress one will admit to anything stop

post interrogation should one survive now fear the gentle sprinkle on a rainy day a pool a shower anything aquatic stop

administration and united nations deem it form of torture stop

Shouting the battle cry of freedom[19]

stop
stop
stop

wonder who the terrorist is

Birth[20]

He emerged with a hair-covered head
(or so they said)
His cry recalled them of the squall
of an orangutan
(or so they thought)
He had one tooth sharp like a fang
(or so they dreamed)
Well-suited
to tear the throats
of their beloved poodles
(or so they feared).

> In the nipa hut
> bamboo floor splashed with blood
> and afterbirth,
> Mary could almost imagine
> she was home –
> but the air through the window
> did not smell
> of mountains nor
> did her parents
> stop by in the line of visitors.
> And in the corner
> of her eye, she caught the shadow
> of a parasol, the tip of a white
> leather shoe; the illusion
> broken.

> But Mary
> brought the baby –
> its head still soft and bent
> in that hollow place -
> to her breast.
> And like any other child,
> he suckled.

Suture

Oddities. Body
parts wrapped to be sold
as souvenirs.
Cold fingers
peel mummy layers
undoing the stitch.

It is invasive,
a sort of jigsaw-
suture the way
Navajos and Igorottes,
Rajasthanis pose
with elephants
at the artificial
Pueblo Cave Dwelling.
You note the backdrop
of painted sand pillars;
that Disneyland
cirrus cloud sky.

Wool jackets rub
loin cloths. Feathers
tickle Victorian necklines.

Hands sew together
what does not belong.
One day, it will heal
into something unrecognizable
with the parts of a person:
a teratoma
with teeth, hair and nails.

Come upon these
measured feet,
this list of names
without warning.
Come from thousands of miles
to witness the exhibit
of the exhibit. Come
to participate in
something, for
your own story does not
allow you to participate.

The candidness of naked
eyes, bare chests devoid
of goosebumps. The smoothness
of distance. The shadows
of the uncaptured. Something
tells you to stop looking,
but you are spun: sutured
to your subject.

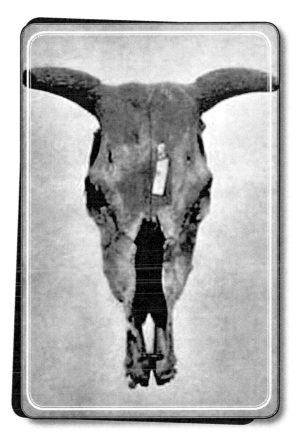

EXHIBIT C: SCIENCE

And that claim is by the right of our manifest destiny to overspread and to possess the whole of the continent which Providence has given us for the development of the great experiment of liberty and federated self-government entrusted to us.

- John O'Sullivan, from "Annexation" in the *Democratic Review*, July-August 1845

Catalog of Names

Abay: next to   (Ilocano)

So many early Christianized Filipinos named themselves after the saints that it caused consternation among the Spanish authorities.[21]

My grandparents named my mother after Eleanor Roosevelt.

Abiog (abyog):   swinging (Tagalog)

Apparently, Christianization worked much too well and there were soon too many Santoses, San Joses, San Antonios, and San Buenaventuras.

Adlao: day (Boholano)

She likes the Beatles song, Eleanor Rigby, and will spontaneously sing it to you by request.

Abog: sudden (Tagalog)

On November 21, 1849, Governor General Narciso Clavería ordered a systematic distribution of family names for the natives to use.

Her middle name, Juana, came from her grandmother, Bae Juana Aning Sur. Bae is short for "Babae", or woman.

Agdeppa: to spread one's hands (Ilocano)

My father was named after Emilio Aguinaldo, who fought for Filipino sovereignty.

Ampon (Ampong): foster child (Tagalog)

Through this system, the Catalogo Alfabetico de Apellidos, approved names were assigned to families in all towns.

Fructuoso – fruitful - was both his father's and his brother's name.

Aoanan: to deplete   (Ilocano)

Because of the mass implementation of Spanish surnames in the Philippines, a Spanish surname might not necessarily indicate Spanish ancestry

> Atabay: wait (Tagalog)

and can make it difficult for Filipinos to accurately trace their lineage.[22]

And as for me: Eleanor and Emilio looked in THE NEW AGE BABY NAME BOOK.

> Awa: mercy (Tagalog)

Aimee means *Beloved* in French. Saint *Bernadette*: the illiterate farmer's daughter who saw an apparition of the Virgin Mary in rural France.

> Awitan: singing (Tagalog)

> Ayuyang: gathering place (Ilocano)

> Avila: a province of central-western Spain (Spanish)[23]

> Arevalo: a municipality in Spain situated in the province of Avila (Spanish)

The words hang upon me like someone else's clothes.

SCIENCE

Two college kids found Kennewick Man in the silt on the banks of the Columbia River. THE "FOUNDER OF ANTHROPOLOGY", JOHANN F. BLUMENBACH Cranial measurements were taken to determine FIRST CLASSIFIED HUMANS INTO FIVE RACES his origins. They AFTER THE FLOOD, HE CONCLUDED, PEOPLE likened his skull to the actor who played Capt. Jean-Luc Picard on Star Trek. *THE CAUCASIAN MUST, ON EVERY PHYSIOLOGICAL* Some said, "Was someone here before the Native Americans?" *BE CONSIDERED AS THE PRIMARY OR INTERMEDIATE OF THESE FIVE PRINCIPAL RACES.* AFRICANS WERE GOVERNED BY WHIMSY, and people went wild, theorizing that the white man may have been here first. ASIANS WERE RULED BY OPINION, *but these bones need proper burial, said* the Umatilla, Yakama, Nez Perce and Colville: AND CAUCASIANS, BY REASON. *Let's put him to rest already. CRANIA AMERICANA,* 1839, DISPLAYED THE INVESTIGATIONS OF SAMUEL GEORGE MORTON *but the bones need further study,* said scientists. *He doesn't fit the Native American profile.* USING MORE THAN 1,000 SKULLS. My father always likes to remind me: **when you were born, your head was deformed** RESURRECTIONISTS WERE GRAVE ROBBERS **because they took it out with forceps. I said, "oh no!"** ACCORDING TO HIS STUDY **and you came out with a crooked head** FROM SIZE OF SKULL, WHICH DETERMINED MENTAL CAPACITY, CAUCASIANS ARE SUPERIOR **but then you came out fine.**[24]

Manifest Destiny 1980

In 1980, two young immigrants and their four-year-old daughter
leave Leonia, New Jersey in a shiny red Saab

> In 1803, President Jefferson asked
> Meriwether Lewis and the Corps of
> Discovery to map a route to the
> Pacific:

They head West for fabled Dream to manifest.
Golden arches and golden streets: antidotes for what was left behind.

> *The commerce which may be carried on with*
> *the people inhabiting the line you will pursue,*
> *renders a knolege of these people important.*[25]

Father lost to the plane bomb.
Brother to the war.
The fear of martial law.
The stubborn lychee tree.
A barren coconut grove.
The sting of salt
and Mamang's kiss.

All fade under this American sun
into the dry, alien horizon.

> *You will therefore endeavor to make yourself*
> *acquainted, as far as diligent pursuit of your*
> *journey shall admit,*

Seat belt holds girl in place
as wind from rolled-down windows
blows her jagged bangs like wings

> *with the names of the nations & their*
> *numbers; the extent & limits of their*
> *possessions;*

Garden State Parkway to the I-80
Indiana, Illinois, Wisconsin, Minnesota,
North Dakota, Montana, Wyoming, Idaho

> *their relations with other tribes or nations;*

The three travelers tread West
towards the Pacific

their language, traditions, monuments;

Little girl dozes on black foam cushions
sun angling through tinted windows
coats her back with sweat.

She dreams they are flying
over continents.
She dreams scenes from Apocalypse Now
and M*A*S*H:
dew-tipped palm fronds,
brown sooty bodies
shadowed in the bush.

it will be useful to acquire what knowledge
you can of the state of morality, religion and
information among them,

Little girl stirs to see the great outdoors:
black asphalt stretched ahead
like an empty chalkboard.

as it may better enable those who endeavor to
civilize & instruct them,

The three travelers move West
pausing at Motel 6's, Denny's,
Arby's, rest stops -
the only Filipinos on these roads.

to adapt their measures to the existing notions
& practices of those on whom they are to
operate

Little girl feels herself change,
four years pushing out the soles
of her little feet.

Black hair expands;
eyelashes thicken,
as signs grow large, then small
states entered and exited.

In all your intercourse with the natives treat
them in the most friendly & conciliatory
manner which their own conduct will admit;

She longs to free herself of the seatbelt,
taut around her waist.

She longs to fly, arms balancing out
rolled-down windows
as they plunge forward

marking land
marking time.

It was cherry pie

that arrived on our doorstep in Kennewick,
the Chalet-style house on 53rd Avenue
on the hill surrounded by tumbleweeds

and snakes and feral cats crouching
in the grass. Back then, Dad was still friendly -
didn't tell us to avoid the door,

his favorite mantra,
"don't trust anyone!"
not yet buried in my 5-year-old ears.

This was before all of that.
This was when Dad and Mom
had kinky blowout perms

that made a shadow
in passport photos
and Sis wasn't even born yet.

And I hadn't discovered Madonna
and I still listened to Annie and Cinderella records
while reading full-color sleeve booklets.

And Dad hadn't joined
the NRA and got all those guns and rifles
he took photos of on their king-sized bed.

We were Daet / Mangaldan / Manila /
Niagara Falls / Maryland / New Jersey
-ites in cherry & apple country.

And this was our first cherry pie
at a time when people still did things like that:
greeted new neighbors with a pie.

And doors were not locked.
And you waved hello to everyone

strolling along the Columbia River.

And the kid with tousled,
dirty blonde hair and apple-
freckled cheeks, asks the new kid in town,

"Hey. Do you wanna play?"

Fun on the Frontier

We wore white cowboy hats dyed with a fluorescent blue, silver-buckled, tucked
with a blue feather. We wore St. Patrick's tee-shirts and bright colored shorts.
Matching.

She was picture-perfect with the rim of the hat tilted over the tip of a tall nose.
The kind of nose I wanted, so I squeezed and pulled hard when no one watched.

She had freckles like Strawberry Shortcake and a smile that made her eyes turn
upside-down moons, dimples. I would smile so hard to punctuate my face.

I painted freckles on one year to be Pippi Longstocking. I had a pug nose, cute
according to. Skin brown like cocoa, even out of the sun. Chubby cheeks.
Short hair, too thick.

I wore knee-highs and keds that soiled easy. Wanted cowboy boots but Mom
never got them. Jelly bracelets up my arm like Madonna. A cowgirl-Material Girl.

Inside, we petted goats as eyes grew veils of dust. The goats were itchy and smelled
like wet dogs. We rode teacups, holding our brims. Screamed "yee-haw!"

Mom lingered as we pretended we were old enough to be alone. I felt apologetic
for her accent and our general hue. She bought us pink and blue cotton

candy and we ate it too fast. Bought us tokens so we could use the mechanical
hand to never get the stuffed animal. On the way out, we screamed "yee-haw!"
linking arms

and Mom took a picture.

My Dad, the Filipino Cowboy
A Split Couplet

He had a silver gun upon his hip.
No one could slip.

A silver car with license: "KNIFE," his horse.
And even worse,

He smoked cigars. Or maybe cigarettes,
but you can bet

He was the talk of town, a brown man
who could stand

without the validation of a white man.
He has the hands

of a baby, soft and thin, I guess
a surgeon's blessed.

But picture Dad, a doctor with a silver
gun, and were

he not the shyest man you ever met,
you'd be upset.

Guns & Satin Sheets

Next to the bed
  in the drawer
  pushed towards the back
  sleeps a small pistol
  in case of emergency.

I tiptoe with caution,
  as though I might let off a bullet
  with the shudder of my thought.
  I pass my hand over the pink satin comforter
  and the cold brass rails of the bed.

Madonna's "Like a Virgin" jostles in my headphones
  plugged into the bright yellow waterproof
  Sony cassette player.

Dad goes to the firing range
  with his buddies Sem and Serg.
  He seems to come back
  taller and broader,
  laughter studded with a bit more swagger.

Then he and his buddies burn through Marlboros
  tossing back stout glasses of scotch whiskeys
  (It's not whiskey, it's scotch!)
  sitting in the linen couches in the "music room"
  gathered round the sharp-cornered coffee table
  that once gave me a gash
  that sent me to the hospital.

The angled high ceilings fill up
  with airy sounds of Chopin or Kitaro or the early Beach Boys
  or the soundtrack to the Clockwork Orange
  (I sometimes sneak a look at the picture sleeves:
  naked woman among a gang of men.
  that one dark eyelash and delirious smile.)

How far away from the life in Daet, Bicol

the dirt roads where slim men stroll in tsinellas,
windows open to the lamok buzzing drunk
on heat and blood.

And the lizards skittering into the rafters,
cockroaches measuring the wall, antennae
like fencing swords, ticking this way and that.

How far from the roosters crowing 6 am, 10 am and 4 pm
the rusty creak of pedicabs, passengers in an aluminum egg
as the breeze tickles their dewy cheeks
driver's knees and muscled calves
catching sun.

How far the guns and the satin comforter
the high ceilings, Kitaro's *Cosmos* riding
trails of Marlboro smoke -
how far the Scotch glasses diamoned with ice

from the crackle of film at Cine del Sol.
The coffee-can popcorn tins
and the scared little boy who held on
to his father's leg as the storm raged,
the lychee tree and the sturdy leg
his shelter.

The lungs are essential
With found text from *Gray's Anatomy*

the lungs
are essential
organs of respiration
taking in
and translating
the ethereal
into word

they are two
in number
like two lovers
curled together
placed one
on either side
within the thorax

separated
by the heart
and other contents
of the mediastinum

it floats in water
crepitates when handled
owing to the presence of air
in the alveoli

the lungs
are essential.
they are two
in number

they are highly
elastic
their surfaces
smooth;
shining.

Scissor-cut

At the big house on 53rd avenue
    at the top of the hill
    in front of the desert where everything died
    Joy and I were hanging out.

She was in the big bathroom with the skylight
    at the end of the hall
    when I heard her cry.

Suddenly feeling like the grown up,
    I rushed towards her. Why
    was she playing with scissors -
    what was she trying to cut?

And more importantly, why
    did I give these scissors
    to another 8-year-old?
    For these were not the *normal* kind,
    but the so-sharp, pointed surgical scissors
    brought home by Dad
    from Our Lady of Lourdes.

I always complained
    that we didn't have *normal* scissors
    in the mug in the kitchen
    with the pencils and the clicky pens
    like *normal* families did.

And why at dinner time, Dad
    would be sitting in the living room
    watching surgical tapes on Beta Max

and I'd catch someone's stomach
    opened up, yellow and shining
    with blood and saline, wishing
    we could switch to Nickelodeon
    or the Care Bears or Pee-Wee Herman.

But there were many things we did
    that weren't *normal*.

Like putting out the sili and the Jufran,
    not ketchup
    to sop up with fried bangus, and never
    bread or salt, but rice and soy sauce.

Or how I'd pronounce "war" or
    prepare to hear *arrai!* if Dad stubbed a toe,
    or got pricked with a fish bone;
    never *ouch!*

Or how I never had grandparents around
    just the excited tone in my mom's dialect
    salty and oceanic
    on a long-distance call
    before she returned to say:
    Aimee! It's your Lola!

Joy faced the toilet, nursing her finger.
    The underside was unbearably yellow
    against the deep brown of the top of her hand.

It had been nicked
    and the blood bubbled into a perfect orb
    like a world contained.

It was almost beautiful.

I stared for a long moment
    before I got responsible
    going to mom for a band-aid.

Joy's brows pinched together
    her brown eyes bulging;
    she bit her lip, thinking
    her finger might fall off.

And her thick braids, closed

with the little balls
that reminded me of marbles
swung like pendulums. *Joy!*

I chided, thinking I was so mature.
    Don't be such a baby.

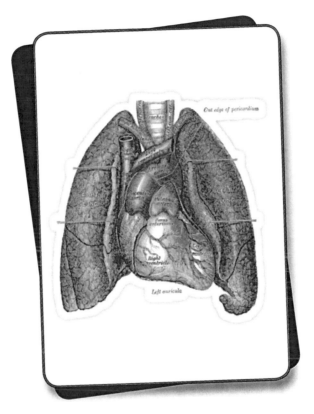

EXHIBIT D: OBJECTS & ARTIFACTS

What determines me, at the most profound level, in the visible, is the gaze that is outside.

– Jacques Lacan, Seminar One

Downwind: A Timeline

1943

> Manhattan Project is in full swing.
> Plutonium is produced at the Hanford Reservation.
> Fuel for the atomic bomb - for the atomic age.

1981

> *Welcome to the Tri-Cities!*

We're ragged and raring after the road trip West.
We trace the path of Lewis and Clark.
Upon arrival in Kennewick, I wonder why Auntie Jess
had to get both of her breasts taken out.

As a welcome gift, we get a jar of Mt. St. Helen's ashes.
The sunsets are spectacular.

> *Hydroplanes!*
> *County Fairs!*
> *The Blue Angels!*

Nukes are all the rage. Clean, powerful, safe.

> *Shop at Atomic Foods!*
> *Stroll down Proton Avenue!*
> *Cheer for the Bombers!*

In second grade, we take a tour of the Hanford Reservation.
Our souvenirs: brown irradiated marbles in little paper pouches
like the ones you put your baby teeth in after they fall out.

We roll the cold orbs in our palms.

1981

My parents take me jogging along the Columbia River.
They buy matching blue tracksuits and stop eating steak.
New diets cut out Filipino dishes, but encourage Lean Cuisine.

Our first microwave rumbles as the glass dish clunks on rotation.
We watch despite warnings to keep distance. Radiation may be dangerous.

There's something in the water.

My mouth salivates every time I hear the peel of cellophane. Like a cat drooling at the sound of the aluminum can being carved open.

1984
At 8, I dream of becoming the first woman to land on Mars.
I read a book about space colonies and imagine leaving the Earth.

1986
9 nuclear reactors at Hanford are shut down, but I don't know or care.
I hear murmurs of jobs being lost, people suddenly leaving town.

Through my headphones, I hear "Like a Virgin" and the Thompson Twins on cassette, ride my banana-seat pink bicycle, have slumber parties and play hopscotch. On hot summer days, we wade ankle-deep in the cool Columbia River.

1994
I'm in college when I get the phone call. *Your mom has breast cancer. Come home.*
Mom survives after a mastectomy. A jagged line, purple, perforates the skin.

1999
I live for three months near the former U.S. Military base at Clark, Philippines. Learn of miscarriages, cancers, deformities from the benzene, toluene, petroleum byproducts. I live with Crizel, a six-year-old with leukemia. She draws apple trees and angels. We draw together and play dolls. I see a dead body for the first time. An unfinished wooden coffin; the woman I'd met days before, bloated, wrapped loosely with gauze.

2000
Crizel dies on a boat, making headlines. I write poems and speak out about the military industrial complex. She becomes the angel in her drawings, the angel with long hair, surrounded by butterflies.

2001
Twenty years after leaving, I find Kennewick in a book about Superfund sites.
I read about government cover-ups:
> *750,000 gallons of radioactive waste leaked from the plant.*

I learn of a lawsuit: dozens of cancer patients sued the government.
The cost of cleanup would be double the cost of US public education.

I read that: *Canisters spew radioactive steam daily.*
                                Workers keep clear in case of explosion.
                                Strontium-90 is found at 500 times federal standards
                                Thyroid cancer-causing radioactive iodine-131
                                contaminates infants and children.
                                Water-cooled plutonium reactors gather toxins.
                                Native tribespeople are subjected the most
                                due to their fish diet.

Back in the Tri-Cities, Bombers cheer
to the backdrop of the mushroom cloud
painted across their school wall.

Sometimes we would find bones

1.
Sometimes we would find bones
up the hill where lots stayed abandoned always
past the haunted house we walked by quickly without looking up
     (once I did and thought I saw a white woman waving).

Once it was a horse's head, I guessed,
it was long and had large eye-sockets   or maybe a dog, I would not know the
difference
I was nine did not yet know these things.

2.
At dinner times, the TV screen flashed red and flesh and sinew.
Dad watched procedures, marking every move
each fine gesture,   the scalpel, scissors, incision, insertion, the swabs, the
                careful sew, the breathing, undulating flesh, yellowish
                surfaces bulging and billowing, almost graceful, the
                viscous fluid coating everything, the
yellow hands, the latex

This was a family tradition

3.
just like the tree we bought every year
we swathed with red satin balls as Boone, Crosby,
Presley hummed thin and warm from the record player
I'm dreaming of a white...Christmas...
(no *kundiman* in Tagalog, no *pancit* or *lumpia*,
we sliced turkey and cylinders
of canned cranberry),
this was all-American

4.
like Sandy, who always had
Orville Redenbacher and M&M's ready at the door and
when we arrived she brought us Apple Pie   she had

a million little kittens and a banana slide and dirty blonde hair and her Dad
reminded me of
Huey Lewis   sometimes

her little brother Randy tagged along on expeditions
up the empty road where lots harbored couches   and random rusted metal parts.

5.
We passed the pile of white things,
the gaping head   the green couch with paling
drooping upholstery,
the wooden frame, innards   exposed, we trudged
100-degree heat   tingling   no clouds   no trees   no seaborne breeze
up the barren steaming strip   yellow pac-man dashes   waving.

They left us changed.
We felt the lightness of time
skinny legs casting shadows that grew as we did.

There in the desert
we watched seasons pass.
We watched birds die   and kittens too.

Dad and the Lychee Tree

Sometimes, Dad freezes his hand into a fist.

What do you brace, so as not to break?

35 years ago   the quick escape
elope   hope of
        hand rests on Bible
        as they name Presidents, States.

                              Later on duty for 17-hour shifts
                              he studies under the best of surgeons
                              4 hearts and 2 aneurysms a day

Dream becomes   windows grow dark as Saab pulls away

What do you brace, so as not to break?

Father grasps the breath that lungs reject
a machine called "bi-pap" gives him air

Mom used to wake him in the fight of night.
            It was still and so
            was my father's chest.

        He recalls:
        The solitary lychee tree   leans
                from the *baguio* brewing   an approaching cracking
                    five-year-old Dad, reed in the snap of wind
                        Lolo Fructuoso's capacious arm
                        shadow falls over the young limbs
                        of the plant promise of fruit

        This is how the story goes.
        This is before the explosion
        sends Lolo down from the sky
        leaving Dad and five siblings fatherless
        the curled fist of big brother -
        unwelcome substitute.

It must have been the skinny lychee tree
and the patriarchal leg, Dad's shelter from a storm.

What do you brace, so as not to break?

My Mother's Watch

I.

My mother's watch:
a two-toned, gold-band Rolex.
Small, moon-like face encased in
curve of heavy glass -
time measured without numbers.

At the *palengke* in the rural province
I say
> *Mom, that's too flashy.*
> *someone might try to rob you.*
I heard that Tito R. got stabbed in a dark alley
near the house in Manila
for a fake Rolex
with a too-shiny gold band.

> Its tiny hands tick time
> almost imperceptibly.

Doesn't she notice
no one else in the *palengke*
is wearing a real Rolex?
Instead, pseudo-American logos tattoo polyester tee shirts,
old housedresses fade in the humidity.
Doesn't she notice
shifty gazes from low-moving youngsters
slip through the narrow spaces between the
bangus stand overflowing with gravels of ice
and the bushels of tumbling green bananas
and the meat hanging in flanks, swaying slightly?
> I see
> that the vendors eye us curiously,
feeling our fidgety ways as they hawk their goods,
my height uncanny despite
hunched-over shoulders -
unflattering blouse to hide my curves.
And the recognition of us Americans like spies

causes a shift in tongue:
They quickly switch
from Pangasinense or Ilocano
into Tagalog,
Taglish, and finally, English
Bili na kayo! Yessss Ma'am, Sir…

II.

My mother's watch:
emblem of 1969
20 borrowed bucks   secret wedding
two twenty-somethings gawk out the window as they descend
into the mouth of the Big Apple.

The newlyweds
learned to cook gizzards, necks and smelt,
occasionally *adobo* as a treat.
First TV: a gift carried on his lap from port of entry to Niagara Falls.

America:
        unrecognized credentials
lawyer uncle turned butcher to feed his eight children
        couch-surfing and loans
                six to a bedroom: *like a can of anchovies*
                caffeine and anemia   not enough sunshine
                        untreated TB and pneumonia
                                memorizing of books to pass exams while
                        memories of home melt into
                too many cups of instant coffee.

III.

A child's Fisher Price record player
tinkles "Mary Had a Little Lamb."
Dad flips real vinyl on Technics. We learn
Beatles, Beach Boys and Benatar.
Late nights sleepy-eyed after emergency room calls:
the garage door opens.

Ice *clinks* in a whisky glass.

IV.

They do not yet miss their left-behind lives:
    Lolo's rule in the house with the green metal gate where
    nine kids left for the West,   one by one by one
        movie house in the little town by the sea
        popcorn sold out of recycled coffee cans
        Sine del Sol burns to the ground:
        fatherless ten   sibling grudges

tsinellas shuf shuf shuffle across aged wooden floors
time   measured in sunrise and sunset

                The ones left behind keep time in slow
                tick tock the clocks not turning digital

                    send us some Tang, cigarettes, M&Ms
                    medicine, a change of the curtains

V.

Now we are too fat and too fancy
standing in the *palengke*
flies hover over mounds of silvery anchovies
jackfruit is cracked open to reveal orange innards
durian sends pungent soursweet towards our nostrils
      time   measured in the melting of ice, the rotting of fruit.

I feel ashamed for the fat on my cheeks
try to disappear, but an American can be seen   from miles away.
And Mom refuses
to hide her real Rolex
even when a watch
is unnecessary.

because going home is not always romantic

and even though it is in fashion to be mixed blood and/or light skinned and/or ethnically ambiguous and/or kinky-haired and light skinned and/or dark skinned and straight-locked and/or with an unidentifiable accent and/or checking the box that says decline to state   I have been called Pocahontas by a little white kid and let me estimate 29 times asked if I am Native American and 23 times Hawaiian and 19 times Tibetan or Indian and now let me forget the times I was asked almost accurately but then sometimes I wished I really was those other things that's the funny thing

and even though its all about going to our roots and mango trees and banana leaves and coconuts and avocado oil for healthy hair and skin and eating crabs with your fingers pre-Spanish fork and spoon and pre-KFC native chicken you can be served by dancing feathered natives that is true it all tastes good but really there is also the glue-sniffing children with no shirts hawking towels cross-cut with twelve year old strippers red lights beer bellied white men gawking cross-cut with high rise proper English speaking businessmen with Spanish names wives applying bleached skin products sold on every counter is not very romantic I assure you.

The Heart is a Hollow

O sax player with a jail needle tattoo…call my lonesome tempest heart, its buried mother's kiss,
bless us in staccato… - Juan Felipe Herrera, from "Iowa Blues Bar Spiritual"

I.
Definition of a Heart
With found text from *Gray's Anatomy*

the heart is a hollow muscular organ
of somewhat conical form

it lies between the lungs
is enclosed in the pericardium
is placed obliquely in the chest
behind the body of the sternum

it lies
sometimes
scar tissues
its own ruptures
it toughens
like a glove
when siphoned out

it swells
not from too much affection
but from consuming
too much sugar

II.
How to resurrect a dying heart

Un-fall into a coma.
Return the breath to lungs.
Un-traumatize.
Return the heart to its innocent state.
Reflesh the bones.

III.
Suspended animation

During open heart surgery, the heart is stopped. Then the science of buying time.
He only has 45 minutes. Normally the brain would die in 5. Cold blood is pumped
into dead veins. Brain is kept on ice. This is called suspended animation. Slow
motion. Cells are not dying but remain in stasis. Similar to sirloin steaks sent to
the freezer. Now the heart is repaired with scalpel, scissors, needle, thread. The
flatline like an egg timer. Only 45 minutes before the cells realize the heart is not
pumping. The surgeon finishes with 7 minutes to spare. All animation is returned
to the organs; ventilation through the respirator machine. Warm blood journeys a
tube. The heart thrums back into beat.

Tiny fires

Listen.
We   *butiki* slid bulbous bellies
          over smooth rocks   we

gentle *butanding*
turned the sea into milk.

Now   Nestle carton bobs
on the fetid waters of the Pasig.
          Open sewers gape   like torn bellies.
Children hunt
for metal parts and plastic sacks.   *Pandacan*
birthed poets, but now it sits
in the shadow of a fuel tank   *ripe for disaster.*
                        (Unassailable evidence)
Obtuse CEOS gaze down metallic towers
cursing shanty dwellers   clicking mahjong/kicking sipa/butchering pigs
in the hell below.

We   bloodstain *tutubi*
          wings thirty feet spanned,
could be seen drifting between storms and songs.
We   30,000 eyes   began with gills
in shallow edges
of the river.   Could breathe underwater.

I tell you this because the thing is happening and you may look upon your cracked
sheaths and see a thing that we were not. You may call yourself John/Susan/Kate
wear Old Navy smile when someone thinks you look like Brad/Jennifer/Angelina.
You may tip cowboy hats, sling guns on hips, shift the gears of German sports cars.
But one day the game is up:

The ones who gave you compliments regard your eyes
detect your bloodstain wings pressing through your skin.

This is why it is important
that you listen

and remember   we were not
jars of talcum powder.
        Not Master Creams and syringed serums cramming
drugstore aisles.
        Not teenaged strippers in red-light districts with faraway looks,
waiting for the 'Kano to take us home.

Not the Aeta woman begging at the edge
of the landfill
where tiny methane fires light up the mountains
of what the world has tossed away.

We   *butanding*
We   *butiki*
We   *tutubi*
          could breathe underwater.

NOTES

[1] In 2011, the American Association for the Advancement of Science held a conference examining the United States World's Fairs in San Diego, CA.

[2] These are actual names of Filipinos on living display at the Exposition. From *Anthropology Goes To the Fair* by Nancy Parezo and Don Fowler, 2007.

[3] From *The Forbidden Book* by Abe Ignacio, Enrique de la Cruz, Helen Toribio, and Jorge Emmanuel.

[4] On May 26, 1900, Private Humbleton wrote: "Our fighting blood was up, and we all wanted to kill 'niggers.' This shooting human beings is a 'hot game' and beats rabbit hunting all to pieces" (*The Forbidden Book*).

[5] The words of a British observer of the US conquest of the Philippines, from Noam Chomsky's "Deterring Democracy."

[6] Text from Paul Kramer's *The Blood of Government: Race, Empire, the United States, and the Philippines.*

[7] Actual text from the Pear's Soap ad, 1899.

[8] Primary source on display at the Missouri History Museum.

[9] Transcriptions of William Link's interview, courtesy of the Missouri History Library.

[10] Text from archival materials written in 1904, courtesy of the Missouri History Library.

[11] Testimony of a Filipino who was on exhibit at the 1904 World's Fair, from Jose Fermin, *1904 World's Fair: The Filipino Experience.*

[12] The "Missing Link" referred, first, to a monkey at the Pan-American Exposition in 1901, and then to Ibag, a Negrito Filipino described by anthropologists and fair organizers as lowest on the totem pole of humanity.

[13] From *The Official History of the Fair, St. Louis 1904*, John Wesley Hanson.

[14] "The easiest way to establish a new norm, such as the right of preventive war, is to select a completely defenseless target, which can be easily overwhelmed by the most massive military force in history. However, in order to do that credibly…you have to frighten people." - Noam Chomsky, from "Imperial Ambition," an interview by David Barsamian.

[15] From Rudyard Kipling's poem, "The White Man's Burden," in *McClure's Magazine*, 1899.

[16] "Men visitors were invited to join the dance which they frequently did, borrowing the tom-toms while the owners sat watching and laughing at their attempts to execute the peculiar Igorrote gyrations…if the dancer was successful, he was rewarded by cries of 'good boy, good boy' from the Igorrotes, who found great enjoyment in watching the dance," from *Anthropology Goes to the Fair.*

[17] Antero was one of the Igorottes who became an intermediary and helped Fair curator William Jenks bring a group on tour; they were popular at the Alaska-Yukon Exposition of Seattle, 1909.

[18] From the *Missouri Historical Society Bulletin.*

[19] Text in italics from an U.S. Army marching song written during the Philippine-American War

[20] "An Igorrote baby was born during their seven-month stay and contemporary accounts of its birth had the tone of a new baby animal at the zoo." – Henry Iglauer, 1904.

[21] Text from Hector Santos' *Katálogo ng mga Apelyidong Pilipino (Catalog of Filipino Names).*

[22] Text from Wikipedia.com.

[23] Names from Hector Santos' *Katálogo ng mga Apelyidong Pilipino (Catalog of Filipino Names).*

[24] Source of information in capitals is from *Anthropology Goes to the Fair.*

[25] All italics in the right-hand column are actual text from the letter from Jefferson to Lewis, 1803.

ABOUT THE AUTHOR

Poet and playwright Aimee Suzara's published work includes her chapbook *the space between*, nominated for the California Book Award, and poems and articles in *Lantern Review*, *Kartika Review*, *580 Split*, Tea Party Magazine, Filipinas Magazine, and the anthology *Walang Hiya (Without Shame)*: *literature taking risks towards liberatory practice*. She is a Hedgebrook and Atlantic Center for the Arts alumna and her theater work has received grants from the National Endowment for the Arts, East Bay Community Foundation and others. A graduate of the Mills College M.F.A. program, she currently teaches Creative Writing and Social Action at California State University at Monterey Bay as well as several San Francisco Bay Area colleges. Suzara has performed her poems nationally and is passionate about teaching creative writing with a social action lens to young people and adults. Her mission is to create, and help others create, poetic and theatrical work that evokes dialogue and social change. www.aimeesuzara.net

CPSIA information can be obtained
at www.ICGtesting.com
Printed in the USA
FSOW01n1044220416

9 781625 490636